Dialogue
with a
Donkey

Stephen Bishop

Published by Zaccmedia
www.zaccmedia.com
info@zaccmedia.com

Published February 2014

ISBN: 978-1-909824-25-6

British Library Cataloguing-in-Publication Data
A catalogue record for this book is available from the British Library

CONTENTS

AUTHOR'S NOTE

Not far from where this material was prepared there is a terraced house on which is displayed a blue plaque. It marks the home at one time of James Hilton, author of the novel *Goodbye Mr. Chips*. Unlike that work of fiction (purportedly based on a local grammar school), these few pages are not designed to entertain or inform, although there are hopefully traces of both! Rather, this could better be described as a travelogue. All of us, writer and reader, are on a journey – that of getting to know God better. It is my hope and prayer that something of what is shared under this title, *Dialogue with a Donkey*, will help us experience Him in a more real way.

INTRODUCTION

Voices and conversations surround us. Not only externally but also within, reverberating in the depths of mind and spirit. Studies, such as the findings released by the Maryland University USA in 2013, have indicated that most people speak several thousand words in a single day. By implication we are the recipients of a similar volume, if not greater. A galaxy of technological innovation now adds to the cacophony of sound resulting in 24/7 connections feeding in from all directions. The clamour for attention now seems to constitute a continual battering of our senses.

But what is really being said? Who is actually speaking? How is it that words can have such impact? Why can voices, even from the distant past, wield power? Why do they continue to echo deep within? And where can God be discerned in all of this? Indeed, is He unaware of what is happening, or simply remaining silent?

SPIRITUAL CONVERSATIONS

Essentially, the Bible is to be seen as the Book about voices. It is God's word to humankind. But the **Words are seen** voice of God is not to be understood **to exert control** purely in physical terms. The psalmist was inspired to write: *'Deep calls to deep in the roar of your waterfalls'* (Psalm 42:7). A spiritual dimension is at work. Words are seen to exert control. The Creator of the universe speaks to us. On every page, the Bible is describing His conversations with people.

BALAAM

Among the myriad characters who hear the voice of God in the Bible lurks Balaam, a shadowy figure. His contemporaries did not seem able to understand him. Present-day preachers, generally, seem reticent to focus on him, or struggle to find any positive spiritual applications in his circumstances. Yet essentially he can be seen as a man of voices, physical and spiritual, demonic and divine, audible and unheard. He experiences what all of us have to live through. Many, however, remember him simply as part of an improbable double act, his talking donkey being the other half! But what on the surface may seem a bemusing episode is integral to an ominous series of events involving strange pronounce-ments and enigmatic conversations. It is worth studying his brief appearance in Scripture because we can learn about the impact of words on his life and, through him, to others, all of which can have a bearing on our own experience.

These events concerning Balaam should not be discarded as minor, occupying a handful of chapters, or irrelevant, unsuited for our sophisticated and educated age. That's because we continue to live in an environment of voices, physical and spiritual. We cannot cut ourselves off from them. They determine our future, accompany every step of our lives, and were speaking over us before we were even born.

... we continue to live in an environment of voices...

CREATION

At the beginning of time we read that the first act of God in bringing this world into existence was to speak: 'Let there be light' (Genesis 1:3). Seven further commands are issued, each prefaced: 'And God said...' The psalmist confirmed this means of creation: 'For he spoke, and it came to be; he commanded, and it stood firm' (Psalm 33:9). The culmination of God's work is finally described: 'Then God said: Let us make man in our image, in our likeness..." (Genesis 1:26). And so humankind was formed, specifically having the ability to listen, speak and relate to others.

As people, we also faintly reflect God's creative ability by means of speech. This is through having ideas, plans and imaginative concepts that are expressed in words. These can then be steps towards initiating material change. Thus words are the means to seeing our lives shaped. Again, this is faintly reflective of God's word bringing transformation as described by the apostle Paul: 'the God who gives life to the dead and calls things that are not as though they were' (Romans 4:17). That is why we need to hold on to what God says to us both in general terms as His children, and individually.

OTHER SOUNDS

Through scientific research, we are aware that audible sound is but a small spectrum of the 'noise' that rings around the created universe. Even the simple tasks of tuning an old radio demonstrates that there are unperceived conversations around us all the time. This is but a parable of the spiritual realm. The Bible records that there was *'rejoicing'* and *'delighting'* in the heavenly places when God spoke this world and humankind into being (Proverbs 8:27–31). Subsequently, the angelic host could not restrain themselves when they later witnessed the birth of Jesus at Bethlehem. *'The Word* [becoming]*flesh'* (John 1:14) to effect our salvation warranted their verbal exclamation: *'Glory to God in the highest, and on earth peace to men on whom his favour rests'* (Luke 2:14). Heaven itself resounds with verbal acclamation of Jesus: *'Salvation belongs to our God, who sits on the throne, and to the Lamb'* (Revelation 7:10). Such words of praise and adoration will endure for eternity.

In the meantime, there is assurance that this world is not hung in a remote part of space left to what may seem to be the capricious forces of nature. God continues to speak into His creation through Jesus: *'The Son is the radiance of God's glory and the exact representation of his being, sustaining all things by his powerful word'* (Hebrews 1:3).

DARK VOICES

However, the Bible describes other voices that speak. Job 1 recounts the conversation between God and Satan about this unsuspecting man who *'feared God and shunned evil'* (Job 1:1). He was oblivious to what was taking place in the heavenly realm, but painfully aware of the outcome! But this intervention was not the first time that humanity heard voices apart from their loving Creator.

Satan's first recorded approach was in the Garden of Eden. This was not a physically threatening or visibly dangerous appearance, but rather a subtle verbal exchange. It began with a question. And it aimed to sow doubt in respect of what God had said: '*Did God really say, "You must not eat from any tree in the garden"?*' (Genesis 3:1). The word of Almighty God was being deviously challenged. 'Can He really be trusted? Does He genuinely have your well-being at heart?' It was with good reason that Jesus taught we should be careful in guarding God's word spoken to us. This was because it would be the specific object of attack. We will be tempted to put aside the words spoken by our heavenly Father. Circumstances may cause them to be snatched away, or their growth being choked (see the parable of the sower, Matthew 13:1–15).

WRITTEN AND SPOKEN

In using the term 'God's word' we may inevitably produce an image of the printed Bible. However, this is not necessarily to restrict us to a non-verbal medium. It needs to be taken into account that the King James Version which was authorized just over four hundred years ago was specifically intended to be spoken aloud. Indeed, the final compilation undertaken by seventeenth-century scholars involved different sections of the Scripture being read audibly to the rest of the assembled delegated translators. They then discussed each passage to which they had been listening before proposing and agreeing any amendments.

The Authorized Version was specifically designed to be read publicly in church and careful consideration was given to ensure that those who listened could understand. Moreover, large portions of that version were based on the pioneering work of the visionary William Tyndale almost one hundred years earlier. A gifted linguist, he set out to make the Bible accessible by frequent and dynamic use of monosyllables, such that even the illiterate 'boy that driveth the plough' could know the Bible. As a result, God's voice was once again being heard by the general population through the Scriptures. Indeed, such was the vibrant structure of those words spoken aloud that very many of them have become commonly used phrases today. The broadcaster Melvyn Bragg presented a television documentary on the subject of the King James Bible to mark its four hundredth anniversary. In describing the rhythm and flow of its rich vocabulary and flowing syntax it was clearly evident that he was needing to work hard at restraining his passion for this 'Book of Books', as he described it.

UNSEEN CONVERSATIONS

Now, as a consequence of these many voices, we can find ourselves being pounded with competing and contrary messages. Many of these we simply do not recognize or realize to be significant. So this collection of studies aims at helping us explore some of the dynamics of words encapsulated in this account of Balaam. Then we shall be applying them to our own situations, aided by questions on which to reflect. Through this we may become better equipped to distinguish God's life-changing word. This may prove to be only a *gentle whisper* (1 Kings 19:12). But it will be life-changing, even if coming by way of a donkey!

1

VOICES IN THE BACKGROUND

BIBLE READINGS:
Numbers 13:17–33; Numbers 14:1–12; Deuteronomy 8:1–11

Grabbing a cup of coffee, having arrived early at church one Sunday, my dulled senses were now reinvigorated! Ready to engage with the human race, I looked around for someone with whom to chat. A friend caught my eye and we were soon catching up on things. It was not long before a situation was being described in which some less-than-helpful comments had been aired. Changing tack, reference was then made to some neighbour's children for whom support was being offered. Initially describing them as twins, this was quickly corrected to give their individual names, my informant knowing from experience the effect of being lumped together with a sibling in such a way. Words, recent and past, were clearly making an impression.

This snippet of conversation highlights something of the underlying force of words. The account recorded in Numbers 22–24 describes a series of events 'behind the scenes'. The Children of Israel were, it seems, totally oblivious to what was going on in the background. Yet these unheard conversations were to have a powerful effect on them.

ABRAHAM – HEARING GOD SPEAK

At this point, the Israelites, following many years of wilderness wandering, were close to their destination of the Promised Land. However, stretching back over several centuries, it was words that had shaped their destiny up to this stage.

> Words were an integral part of this 'package'

God had initiated the whole journey: *'Leave your county, your people and your father's household and go to the land I will show you'* had been his instruction to the patriarch Abram (Genesis 12:1). Obedience to what God was saying was to result in blessing both to his descendants and to others: *'I will bless those who bless you, and whoever curses you I will curse'* (Genesis 12:3). Words were an integral part of this 'package'.

The aged Abraham and Sarah became parents specifically arising from what God had said to them: *'Now the LORD was gracious to Sarah as he had said, and the LORD did for Sarah what he had promised'* (Genesis 21:1). Their son, Isaac, himself became a father, this time of twins. Words continued to shape lives: *'By faith Isaac blessed Jacob and Esau in regard to their future'* (Hebrews 11:20). The younger brother, Jacob, becoming a grandfather, continued to understand the power of words by means of spoken blessing: *'By faith Jacob, when he was dying, blessed each of Joseph's sons, and worshipped as he leaned on the top of his staff'* (Hebrews 11:21). He subsequently blessed his immediate offspring who were to become the twelve tribes of Israel (see Genesis 49).

MOSES – NOT GOOD WITH WORDS

God's plan, then, seemed to be thwarted by words from another source. Initially living in Egypt as honoured residents, this status granted to the Israelites changed over time. They were subsequently placed into slavery through fear of constituting a threat. Then their situation deteriorated even more. The ruler of the Egyptians issued a command that looked as if it would spell the end of their race. Pharaoh ordered that midwives were to kill their baby boys. This was followed up with a general command that the babies were to be thrown into the River Nile (see Exodus 1:22). However, there was a particular couple who resisted these words. They were *'not afraid of the king's edict'* (Hebrews 11:23). Their son was Moses. He was to be God's man to bring deliverance.

... Moses identified this as a key factor in God's commissioning of him

Unfortunately speaking and words were not his 'thing'! When, years later in his adult life he met with God at the burning bush, he whined, *'O Lord, I have never been eloquent, neither in the past nor since you have spoken to your servant. I am slow of speech and tongue'* (Exodus 4:10). It is interesting that Moses identified this as a key factor in God's commissioning of him. It was not his experience, education or expertise that was to count, but his ability to express words.

If Moses felt uncomfortable with words, others were not so inhibited! Unfortunately for Moses, they were his compatriots. Also unfortunately for him, they evidenced their skill in his direction with unabated moaning, grumbling and complaining.... over many succeeding years. God's miraculous deliverance from Egyptian slavery under Moses' leadership had involved the parting of the Red Sea. Negotiating this natural obstacle through supernatural intervention had opened the way for what should have been an eleven-day journey. But unbelief at the voice of God in promising them the land of Canaan changed the schedule, somewhat! The Israelites chose to believe the voices of disbelief from ten of the twelve spies sent ahead and whose report included the conclusion: *'We can't attack those people; they are stronger than we are'* (Numbers 13:31).

God's judgment arising from this distrust in His word was severe. The adult Israelites – those over the age of twenty – would not live to enter the Promised Land. But even in those forty years subsequently spent in the desert God showed His kindness and provision. He worked so that their clothes and shoes did not wear out, manna was food from heaven, rocks gushed out water, and His pillars of cloud and fire guided them. Powerful opposing forces were overcome. Eventually they reached the 'home straight'. And in this closing stage, God enabled them to defeat the blocking armies of enemy kingdoms, including those of Sihon and Og.

FINAL DESTINATION

Then they came to Moab. This people-group was located to the immediate east of the land of Canaan. They were actually related to the Israelites. Lot, the nephew of the great patriarch Abraham, had escaped the destruction of Sodom and Gomorrah by the skin of his teeth. His two daughters, however, desperate regarding the lack of men to marry and by which to have families, conspired to remedy the latter by making Lot drunk. Moab and Ben-Ammi were the resultant offspring (see Genesis 19:37,38).

Fast-forward several centuries and out of fear, Balak, the king of Moab, sought a means to counter this advancing *'horde'* of Israelites, whom he envisaged as *'... going to lick up everything around us, as an ox licks up the grass of the field'* (Numbers 22:4). Concluding that military action alone was insufficient, he devised a different strategy: voices – calling a curse upon God's people. Thus the way is prepared for Balaam to enter the scene, adding to the voices and conversations in the background that had already profoundly shaped Israel's past and continued to influence their direction in the future.

OUR WALK

We now need to pause. The apostle Paul wrote that our weapons of warfare were not of this world (2 Corinthians 10:4). That's because, like the Israelites, our walk with God is influenced not necessarily in a physical but – more importantly – in a spiritual sense. This is where words are vital. Voices are being directed at us that impact our minds, emotions and spirits. So we need to be alert to what we have been picking up and absorbing, not only consciously but also subconsciously. The effects, as the king of Moab attempted to achieve through the pronouncements of Balaam, can compound the negative words, or counteract those that have been forming our lives.

> Voices are being directed at us that impact our minds, emotions and spirits

But God is there to remind us as we journey: *'Whether you turn to the right or to the left, your ears will hear a voice behind you, saying, "This is the way; walk in it."'* (Isaiah 30:21). This is an encouragement to us: God's life-shaping word can still be heard and be effective, even when, like those Israelites, we lose our bearings, encounter adversity, or feel overwhelmed.

FOR REFLECTION

1. The account of the Israelites travelling through the desert and up to the borders of the Promised Land (and the subsequent involvement of Balaam) had been influenced by many events. This had included the report of the twelve spies sent ahead of them. What were the details about which they had all agreed (Numbers 13)? What was described by the majority of the spies, on which the Children of Israel focused, and what was the outcome (Numbers 14)?

2. What was behind Caleb's statement to the people following the general report, and then his joint declaration with Joshua when the people said that they wanted to return to Egypt (Numbers 13:30; 14:6–9)?

3. During the wilderness wanderings, the voice of God had also been shaping the direction and attitude of the Israelites. What had He said to them about the importance of Him speaking to them? What practical provision had demonstrated his overall care for them (Deuteronomy 8)?

4. What do you feel have been the major sources of influence in your life in relation to what has been said to you, and spoken about you? Why do you think that voices in the background of your life can still have an effect?

5. What words, spoken to you by others, would you want God to be aware of and to counteract with His assurance?

2

VOICES THAT QUESTION

BIBLE READINGS:
Numbers 22:2–14; 1 Kings 19:13–18; Genesis 3:1–10; Job 40:6–24

'Can your bank match this?' the wording on the advertisement asked as I travelled by London Underground to work early one morning. Putting a pointed question is a frequent ploy often used in modern advertising. This particular advert was designed to reveal something that a consumer may not have previously considered... and being on a Tube train it engaged a somewhat captive audience. As we move on in this account regarding the Children of Israel, we find that God intervenes in a similar, direct way.

Having determined that military strategy was insufficient to overcome the travelling People of God, the king of Moab raised his fears with his neighbours, the elders of Midian. The indication is that it was the latter who pointed him in the direction of Balaam. This man's reputation was international. If you could have Googled the words 'cursing people' in those days, his name would be top of the screen! He was the man whom the Moabites now wanted to head-hunt.

This man's reputation was international.

So a journey was undertaken by high-ranking officials to track him down and summon him from, *'Pethor, near the River'* (Numbers 22:5) that is, the River Euphrates. This may have taken them up to a month to accomplish. They came with a request... and a fee. The former was quite explicit: to put a curse on the people who had *'come out of Egypt ... too powerful for me'* (vv. 5,6). The latter was clearly a substantial sum, gauged by Balaam's subsequent comment upon a second approach being made (see vv. 7,18).

GOD KNOWS THE ANSWER

But all this activity was not unnoticed by the All-seeing and All-knowing God. Having asked the emissaries for time to consider their proposal, it is inferred that Balaam received a night-time visitation from the Almighty. He may have believed in the God of Israel, Yahweh (*the* LORD, 22:8) as simply being one of many deities. The word translated 'God' (v. 9) conveys the aspect of Him being the Creator, but distant God. Nevertheless a conversation takes place. Balaam, the man of voices, has his first recorded encounter with God. It takes the form of a question: *'Who are these men with you?'*

The Bible has many instances of questions being asked. Usually they are between people or from people, directed to God. But here we have an example of God posing the question. This, as in other cases, is not good news! Is there something taking place of which God is ignorant or unaware? Is it a question to which He is ignorant of the answer? Clearly that cannot be the case. The

8

question being asked is something to which He already knows the response... and so does Balaam! God is underlining a point. Balaam needed to understand that the Children of Israel were different and special: *'You must not put a curse on those people, because they are blessed'* (v.12). The following morning Balaam turns his visitors away with a refusal.

ONGOING QUESTIONS

God still asks questions. His probing voice is still highlighting our potential (or actual) waywardness and deficiencies; to point us to His ways and provision. Jesus' ministry often involved focused interaction with people. His questions went to the core of issues: *'Do you want to get well?'*; *'Where have you laid him?'*; *'What do you want me to do for you?'*; *'Where is your faith?'*; *'How many loaves do you have?'* (see John 5:6; John 11:33; Mark 10:51; Luke 8:25; Mark 6:38)

However, the most haunting of God's questions is the very first one recorded in Scripture: *'Then the man and his wife heard the sound of the LORD God as he was walking in the garden in the cool of the day, and they hid from the LORD God among the trees of the garden. But the LORD God called to the man, "Where are you?"'* (Genesis 3:8,9). I wonder what tone of voice was being used? Was God perplexed, caught out, not sure what had happened? Or was He harsh and demanding, requiring an instant reply? The revealed character of God would show that this was a question spoken out of love. He wanted human beings to have close and personal relationship with Him. But that was now broken through humanity's disobedience and self-centredness. His response was to speak judgment and cursing. But this was not all. There was also a foreshadowing of His plan of salvation being worked out – He made garments of skin for Adam and Eve, an animal needing to be slain for such a provision foreshadowing His own Son's death for our salvation (see Genesis 3:21).

GOD'S PURPOSES

Whenever God asks a question, it is always with certain factors in the background. He is in control of every situation and has total power, as Job needed reminding when bombarded by a series of questions from God in respect to nature: *'Can you bind the beautiful Pleiades? Can you loose the cords of Orion? ... Can you pull in the leviathan with a fishhook or tie down his tongue with a rope?'* (Job 38:31; 41:1) Secondly, He has complete clarity with regard to circumstances that exist. Nothing is hidden from His eyes. *'Does he who formed the eye not see?'* asks the psalmist in a somewhat rhetorical question (Psalm 94:9b). And lastly his questions are always asked out of care for people living in this fallen and fallible world.

OUR OWN QUESTIONS

There is a sense in which God uses our own questioning as a means of bringing us back to Himself. The most asked question by people whenever some serious problem or harmful event takes place, whether purely personal or in the public eye, is one word: 'Why?' Even though we live in a sin-sick world where disasters seems to strike both regularly and without restraint, something within us feels that this should not be... this is not what should be happening. Furthermore, even the avowed non-believer feels that God (whose existence they do not acknowledge) has something to answer for (even though they don't know Him in a personal way, so as to be familiar with His character). Heaven then seems to throw that same question back at us: 'Why?' Because only as we then face up to our severe and chronic limitations in understanding do we realize that God is the One to whom we need to turn and submit.

ON GOD'S RADAR

Such was the case with Balaam. The question he found himself being required to answer was not for God's benefit but his own; for him to realize that this situation wasn't like others that he had experienced. When it comes to God, He doesn't ask nice, polite or superficial questions, but penetrating ones pointing to unavoidable answers. Whereas Balaam may have been used to receiving requests to speak curses (suitably remunerated, of course), God's questioning made him see that this one from Balak was not to be accepted. The demonic activity in which he may well have indulged for such purposes on previous occasions was not to be a part of this sequence in summoning up pronouncements. Balaam was made aware that he was firmly on God's radar and, for once, he was not going to have the final say, either literally or figuratively.

> *When it comes to God, He doesn't ask nice, polite or superficial questions...*

Similarly, as we grapple with unanswered questions and unresolved problems, God could be using these as a means of getting our attention. He wants us to be aware that we are still very much on His radar, however distant we may feel that we are from him. Also, like Balaam, we are brought to understand that God has something to say to us over and above what other people may be bringing. He is to have the final word.

This is what the perplexed Israelites found out when God questioned and then reassured them through the prophet many years later. '*Why do you say, O Jacob, and complain, O Israel: "My way* is hidden from the LORD; my cause is disregarded by my God"? Do you not know? Have you not heard? The LORD is the everlasting God, the Creator of the ends of the earth. He will not grow tired or weary, and his understanding no-one can fathom. He gives strength to the weary and increases the power of the weak. Even youths grow tired and weary, and young men stumble and fall; but those who hope in the LORD will renew their strength. They will soar on wings like eagles; they will run and not grow weary, they will walk and not be faint' (Isaiah 40:27–31).

FOR REFLECTION

1. Why do you feel that it is important that we ask, and are asked, questions in respect of deep issues in our lives?

2. What question, given the opportunity, would you want to put to God about this world in which we live?

3. And what question would you put to God about yourself?

4. God is recorded as asking the question: *'What are you doing here...?'* (1 Kings 19:9). Why do you think that He asked it? If He asked you that question now, what would be your response?

5. Jesus' meeting with Peter included the question (put to him three times) *'... do you truly love me...?'* (John 21:15) Why do you think this was asked... and, again how would you have replied?

3

VOICES OF THE UNEXPECTED

BIBLE READING:
Numbers 22:14–35

Leyton Orient is the name of my local football team. Their results mean that they often languish in the lower levels of the Football League. So, following their struggles may not seem a particularly enriching experience. Yet, as with any aspect of life, God may intervene in a way that's 'outside of the (penalty) box'! Events relating to the club in both the distant past and more recently show this to be the case. As a result of considerable research, the origins of the O's (their nickname) have been traced back to the East End of Victorian London – and some former students from a theological teacher training college for nonconformists and Puritans! They were following up a suggestion to form a football team to enable their existing cricket team to be kept together during the winter.

The name of this nascent team was derived from one of them working for the P & O shipping group. Fast-forward many defeats

13

and relegations later (with the occasional success!), and I was given a leaflet for a church men's dinner where a former Orient player was giving his testimony. I was not the only one surprised to learn of his conversion. When he attended the annual club dinner, the chaplain had announced that this born-again Christian was to say Grace, at which point there was an audible gasp since he had been known as a hard-drinking and talking professional.

REPEATED OFFER

God working and speaking in ways we do not expect is not new. As we continue tracing the ways in which Balaam was a man of voices, we find that the king of Moab was not someone easily put off by that initial rebuff. Whether by desperation or vindictiveness against the Israelites, he dispatches a second delegation to Balaam: 'Then Balak sent other princes, more numerous and more distinguished that the first" (Numbers 22:15). The offer is to reward him '*handsomely*' (v. 17) for putting a curse on God's people. Although seeming to refuse this approach point-blank, Balaam nevertheless asks them to remain the night. The Lord then comes to him and allows him to go back with these emissaries. However there is a clear condition: '… *do only what I tell you*' (v. 20).

A THEOPHANY

It is on that journey to Moab that Balaam's donkey recognizes something that this would-be prophet fails to see. This is somewhat ironic. The 'seer' (as a prophet would be called) failing to see! Of greater significance was the identity of the One who was blocking his path: the angel of the LORD. This is a term generally used in the Old Testament to denote a theophany – the Lord Jesus coming to this earth in visible form prior to His actual birth in Bethlehem. Others who had this experience included Hagar

(Genesis 16:7), Abraham (Genesis 22:11), Jacob (Genesis 31:11), and Gideon (Judges 6:11–18).

The description of the angel with a drawn sword, of Balaam consequently bowing low and falling face down in an attitude of worship, and the instruction to speak 'only what I tell you' (22:35) further indicate that this was no ordinary angel (if such a being could be described in this way) but the Lord Jesus Christ Himself. Later, the apostle John was to recount a similar experience with the risen Lord (Revelation 1:12–20).

ANGEL VOICES... AND THAT DONKEY

God may choose to speak to us in particularly supernatural ways – by revelations and visions of angelic beings. They are described as 'ministering spirits' (Hebrews 1:14) who may appear in unobtrusive ways so that they aren't recognized (Hebrews 13:2). Luke's Gospel and subsequent Acts of the Apostles particularly feature these heavenly beings coming to bring messages to God's people.

But back to earth, and sandwiched between Balaam's initial ignorance and subsequent awesome revelation, that donkey speaks. More precisely, she indicates danger. The donkey's actions in turning off the road into a field and, further on, pressing close to a wall, before finally lying down under her rider were none-too-subtle hints that things were not as they seemed!

Balaam's third beating of the poor animal in response to these events results in God opening the donkey's mouth. And, as highlighted in a previous divine encounter, we have a question. Actually, we have three of them, drawing Balaam's attention to this beast's behaviour being inconsistent with its normal compliant nature. Balaam's recognition of this fact is followed by his eyes also being opened to the awesome presence of the angel of the LORD.

A WARNING

The whole episode comes as a warning to Balaam to do as he's been told. God's restraint is evident in that He clearly wasn't going to let the antics of a donkey prevent Him from slaying Balaam if that was His actual intention. The All-seeing God knew that Balaam's motives were not always what they seemed, or what he voiced. Meanwhile, he is sent on his way with the instruction ringing in his ears: 'Go with the men, but speak only what I tell you' (Numbers 22:35). The donkey conversing with Balaam was not a piece of trickery, but God going to very unusual lengths to ensure that He had Balaam's full attention and compliance in what He was saying.

> The donkey conversing with Balaam was not a piece of trickery...

The Almighty God is not limited in the ways that He chooses to communicate warnings, direction and affirmation into our lives. He speaks through nature, as the psalmist graphically described (Psalm 19:1–6), an area that Jesus readily pointed to when teaching His followers: 'Look at the birds of the air ... See how the lilies of the field grow...' (Matthew 6:26,28). He particularly speaks through His written word, which needs to be the foundation on which we determine our walk in life (see Psalm 119). But other means are also used – for example, He chose my non-Christian line manager at work to speak about my need to move to another location within the organization rather than stay where I was and have to do a different job. This I took to be God's direction at that time.

> ... God chooses to speak to us in a personal way...

The very fact that God chooses to speak to us in a personal way should bring us to a place of deep humility and awe. It is therefore not for us to tell God how He should talk to us, but to be sensitive to that *'gentle whisper'*, whatever form that may take (1 Kings 19:11–13).

FOR REFLECTION

1. Why do you think that it is important to have some kind of daily or regular input from reading the Bible as a way of hearing God speak?

2. Why do you feel that it could be helpful to set aside some regular (or irregular) time to simply focus on God (see Luke 10:38–42)? What practical steps can be taken to put aside distractions preventing us from spending such time with God?

3. What part in hearing God speak does our talking to Him have to play (see 1 Samuel 3:1–14)?

4. Why is it important to remind ourselves of God's promises to speak to us in a personal way?

4

VOICES OF
AFFIRMATION

BIBLE READING:
Numbers 23:1–26

THE FIRST MESSAGE

The hi-tech era of smart phones, iPads and GPS could said to have started back in 1844. That was when first use was made of electricity to transmit a message over the horizon. Samuel Morse's electronic pulses may have needed wires to convey their code, but it was a breakthrough from the purely mechanical and visual technology utilized up to that point. And the text of that first message sent from Washington to Baltimore? They were the words taken from Balaam's second utterance over the Israelites: 'What hath God wrought' (see Numbers 23:23, AV).

BEING SPECIAL

The scheme which Balak, king of Moab, had engineered was now in place. Balaam had arrived on the scene and was brought to a place called Kiriath Huzoth (22:39) and then up to the high places

19

of Baal (22:41). This was the vantage point for viewing most of the Israelites camped below. Alongside Balak he participates in the sacrifice to the demonic entity. He then goes 'walkabout' to see what the Lord might want him to say. The Lord most certainly does have something for him to pronounce! There is an indication of a further theophany. The result is not to Balak's liking. Balaam brings a declaration of blessing upon the Israelites from God, emphasizing their distinctiveness apart from the other nations, and then underlining their vastness (23:7–10). He concludes that this was something that he, Balaam, wanted to be a part of.

... AND BEING SECURE

Similar events precede Balaam's second declaration, or oracle, over the Israelites. Balak had clearly been unimpressed with this first effort. Although having had it explained to him by Balaam that he could only speak what God had put in his mouth, Balak had not grasped what this meant. So he summons him to another peak, Pisgah (23:14), where further sacrifices are offered, again being the potential means of divination. Balaam also repeats his previous action of then trotting off to meet the Lord – *'meet with him over there'* (v. 15) – returning with words that are to be spoken. The uniqueness of Israel before God is again highlighted; it is a fact which He will not go back on, but will carry out in terms of blessing. Furthermore the mark of their specialness and His safekeeping is seen in what He has miraculously undertaken for them in their exodus from Egypt – itself a place infested and influenced by the occult, magicians and divination – and protection from such sorcery. It is in this context that those words used by Samuel Morse were

The Israelites were secure in God's blessing upon them

first uttered declaring what the mighty Lord had worked: *'See what God has done!'* (v. 23). The Israelites were secure in God's blessing upon them.

UNHEARD AFFIRMATION

While all of this was taking place, it may be assumed that the Israelites actually heard nothing of these affirmative words at that time. Rather, not only were they the means of putting Balak firmly in his place, but these declarations were also being directed to unseen powers of darkness and evil, indicated by those initial blood sacrifices that had been offered. Balaam acknowledged that he was the mouthpiece, speaking as instructed by God (v. 20; see vv. 5,16). He was declaring the truth over the Israelites when they were in a particularly vulnerable stage of their journey, about to confront their enemies, spiritual and physical, in the Promised Land. But having declared their status and significance before God, even more powerful things were to be said of them as directed by the Lord.

USE OF THE TONGUE

In that context of affirmation it is noticeable that many of the New Testament letters contain teaching on practical living relating to careful use of speech. James brings one of several forthright admonitions: *'With the tongue we praise our Lord and Father, and with it we curse men, who have been made in God's likeness. Out of the same mouth come praise and cursing. My brothers, this should not be'* (James 3:10). Paul writes specifically about the positive aspect of words. Having put on the *'new self'* (Colossians 3:10) we are to *'Let the word of Christ dwell in you richly as you teach and admonish one another with all wisdom, and as you sing psalms, hymns and spiritual songs with gratitude in your hearts to God'* (v. 16).

He adds, *"And whatever you do, whether in word or deed, do it all in the name of the Lord Jesus, giving thanks to God the Father through him'* (v. 17).

Implicit in these instructions is the sad fact that even Christians can slip into such misuse of the tongue, saying things that amount to serious put-downs of our brothers and sisters. This can arise not only because of this behaviour being endemic in the world around us, but also personal deep-seated feelings of insecurity. As a consequence, we feel the need to talk other people down or refuse to acknowledge their status and worth. By doing so we are trying to make ourselves look better than others. Hence Paul's letter to the Ephesians initially sets out the wonderful plan and purposes of God in our lives to bring us to a place of acceptance and value to Him. This is achieved by being made alive in Christ. As a consequence, we are to *'put on the new self, created to be like God in true righteousness and holiness'* (Ephesians 4:24).

Paul then goes on to demand that having established our position of love and worth in the sight of God, there is to be a response on our part. This is to include the following: *'Do not let any unwholesome talk come out of your mouths, but only what is helpful for building others up according to their needs, that it may benefit those who listen'* (v. 29). This is actually reflective of God's heart; for us to hear His affirming words into our lives in contrast to the denigrating, destructive and degrading voices to which we are so often subjected.

GOD'S LOVE

The irony is that those journeying Israelites had been quick to direct negative and noxious words by way of complaining, murmuring and groaning to Moses, who led them those forty years. By implication, this was to God Himself. So why did God go to such lengths to ensure that Balaam didn't take the opportunity to speak cursing; rather, to bring blessings? And why start with these words of affirmation and confirmation of worth? Perhaps it was partly to redress four hundred years of slavery, when these words were noticeably absent. But are we in a better position? We live in a sin-enslaved environment where negative attitude and words abound. This would partly explain why God inspired those New Testament writers to give such clear guidelines about speech. We are to imitate God in speaking blessing and words that build up.

Ultimately, however, our sense of worth and affirmation comes not from special relationships, but from God

> Perhaps it was partly to redress four hundred years of slavery, when these words were noticeably absent

Himself (though parents, spouses and close friends should be avenues through which this flows). God's affirmation of us is not based on our performance, achievement or successes. It is based on us being His unique creation, redeemed for His glory, reflecting His goodness and mercy. God's response to His wayward people, struggling with lack of worth and affirmation, has always been undergirded in love. Many years after Balaam, He spoke through the prophet Jeremiah to a continuing recalcitrant people: 'I have loved you with an everlasting love; I have drawn you with loving-kindness. I will build you up again and you will be rebuilt, O Virgin Israel' (Jeremiah 31:3,4a). Even in our present environment of slander, cynicism, gossip, backbiting and ridicule, God is speaking affirmation and hope, as He did to those unsuspecting Israelites through Balaam.

FOR REFLECTION

1. Why do you feel that it is important to received affirmation of worth and value from parents, schoolteachers and others who have major influence on us?

2. How can we affirm others based on who they are, rather than on what they achieve?

3. What descriptions does the New Testament writer Peter use to affirm his readers (1 Peter 2:9,10)? What other verses can you finding in that chapter which bring affirmation?

4. In addition to speaking, what practical ways can we bring affirmation to those alongside us?

5

VOICES OF THE PROPHETIC

BIBLE READING:
Numbers 24:1–14

There is a marked difference between the remaining declarations
of Balaam, starting with this third one, and the first two. It's
as though he has moved through a gear change in terms of his
perception of what God is saying. The narrative draws attention
to the fact that *'he did not resort to sorcery as at other times, but
turned his face towards the desert'* (24:1). Although sacrifices had
been offered, he made no use of them as a possible source of
demonic inspiration. Indeed, he didn't even go off somewhere to
experience another theophany by which to hear God's instruction
as to what to declare. Instead we are told: *'When Balaam looked out
and saw Israel encamped tribe by tribe, the Spirit of God came upon him
and he uttered his oracle'* (v. 3).

SPIRIT INSPIRED
God the Holy Spirit had not yet come upon God's people
generally. This was to take place many centuries later at

Pentecost and subsequently, as promised by Jesus and specifically prophesied by Joel. Instead, as best as can be understood, He came upon specific people for them to be enable to undertake specific tasks. These included the various judges being able to drive out oppressive forces from Israel, Saul and David in their roles as kings, and then the prophets. Prior to all of these, God had actually moved by His Spirit upon Moses and then placed Him on the seventy elders (plus two others who had appeared to have gone awol!); all had prophesied as a consequence (Numbers 11:25,26).

BALAAM'S DECLARATION

Balaam, having the Spirit of God come upon him, responded by prefacing his declaration with a confession; what he was seeing was a revelation brought by God alone, who was opening his eyes and ears (24:3,4). What Balaam then proclaimed was not derived from his physical sight. On the surface the Israelites were a motley collection of people who'd been wandering around the desert in clothes that had not worn out. Their future prospects were humanly uncertain if not hopeless, they had no home of their own, they could not turn back, and their resources were significantly limited. But God saw them very differently.

What followed could more be appropriately labelled as a prophecy. Balaam was speaking over the Children of Israel a description of how God saw them, not what would have been seen at that time by a human observer: 'How beautiful are your tents, O Jacob, your dwelling-places, O Israel!' (v. 5). Thus commences a series of pictures, and a pronouncement referring to refreshing, blessing and power (vv. 6– 9).

> But God saw them very differently

Not only was this an irresistible retort against King Balak's scheme to bring a curse against the Israelites, they were the words of the Creator God. He was bringing change to a people who previously had damagingly taken the view that they were *'grasshoppers'* (Numbers 13:33). This was the voice of the Lord Almighty: *'God brought them out of Egypt; they have the strength of a wild ox. They devour hostile nations, and break their bones in pieces'* (24:8). This did not match up to their present observable status, but was a revelation of God's heart and plan for them.

PERSPECTIVE

As seen here, 'prophecy' is not so much the predicting of the future before events actually take place, but rather a proclamation of how God views us, both individually and collectively. This Divine perspective is likely to be very different from how others see us, or how we view ourselves. However, as our heavenly Father and the Lord of Hosts, His is the evaluation that we need to hear.

It is the truth about who we really are, not a distorted and maligned assessment. As Balaam testified all those centuries ago,

> ... 'prophecy' ... a proclamation of how God views us...

this is so awesome and powerful that it should cause us to fall prostrate (see v. 4). The proverb boldly states: *'Every word of God is flawless'* (Proverbs 30:5); what we sense is spoken by God is not to be treated lightly.

JUDGING GOD'S WORD

But how are we to judge such a perspective? What should our attitude be towards words of prophecy? By referring to the declarations which Balaam uttered we can establish the means by which we can properly process what we are now hearing from God – the new and different way in which He sees us.

First of all it was underlined that *God is not a man, that he should lie, nor a son of man, that he should change his mind'* (23:19). This indicates that any words that are brought are to be put alongside what is already revealed about God and His character. He is consistent; with Him there is no *'variableness'* (see James 1:17, AV).

Secondly, it needs to be asked whether it is in line with what He has already said about His plans and purposes. Balaam's declarations of blessing upon the unlikely Israelites was entirely consistent with God's previous promises to Abraham, Isaac and Jacob, none of whom had any pretensions of grandeur; God had spontaneously spoken to each of them of His heart for the people who were to descend from them. They were to be a great people through whom the world was to experience indescribable blessing, ultimately to be realized in Jesus, the Son of God. Balaam, possibly ignorant of this history, was entirely spot on. God spoke through Isaiah: *'I made known the end from the beginning, from ancient times, what is still to come. I say: My purpose will stand, and I will do all that I please'* (Isaiah 46:10).

Thirdly, does any word brought reflect upon the ultimate glory of God? Balaam had, in the earlier declaration, pointed out, *'No misfortune is seen in Jacob, no misery observed in Israel. The LORD their God is with them; the shout of the King is among them'* (23:21). What God was speaking over the Israelites was so that others could see His power, glory and love expressed towards people with whom He had chosen to identify. They neither deserved it nor necessarily valued it. Yet He had specifically chosen them to display His unconditional love. And we are very much like those incorrigible and complaining people! Yet God wants to pour out His affection

28

and care towards us so that His glory might be shown all the more through jars of clay (2 Corinthians 4).

PERSONAL PERSPECTIVE

Just as God spoke over the Israelites, so He speaks to us. This can be in many ways, but is always based on His revealed word in the Bible. The problem is that we can be so overwhelmed by the opinions and judgments of others regarding ourselves (and our future) that we feel powerless to focus on God's perspective. How like the Israelites! Trudging through the desert, threatened by powerful enemies, friendless and powerless, and all the time the word 'grasshopper' was at the back, or even forefront, of their minds. Only God's word, that same word that created something out of nothing, that same Word that became flesh to reveal God's self-giving love, can change our perspective to that of God's life-giving truth about us. The Israelites had desperately needed to hear in their hearts, minds and spirits that they were no longer 'grasshoppers' – and never had been. We need to hear the same!

> ... all the time the word 'grasshopper' was at the back, or even forefront, of their minds

In pondering those words declared through Balaam, we glimpse something of God's heart towards us: 'How beautiful are your tents, O Jacob, your dwelling-places O Israel! Like valleys they spread out, like gardens beside a river, like aloes planted by the LORD, like cedars beside the waters' (24:5,6)

This amazing and vivid picture from God through Balaam was indicating a climax in this season of His dealing with His people. He was about to bring them home. His word was about to be realized.

We can experience a similar homecoming to God's destiny for us as we receive His life-enhancing word into our lives.

FOR REFLECTION

1. What different influences may cause us to have a low self-esteem? Why can these impact us so deeply?

2. What can be some of the effects of not having a right perspective of who we are and what we can achieve, with God's help? How did this effect work itself out in the case of the Israelites (see Numbers 13:26–33)?

3. What steps can be taken to have a better understanding of how God sees and thinks of us?

4. What lessons can be drawn from the account of Caleb, who didn't hold to the 'grasshopper' mentality, when he finally ended up in the Promised Land (see Joshua 14:6–13)?

6

VOICES THAT POINT TO JESUS

BIBLE READING:
Numbers 24:15–19

Our God contracted to a span,
Incomprehensibly made Man.

So wrote Charles Wesley (1707–88) in one of his great hymns ('Let Earth and Heaven Combine'), trying to encapsulate what it meant for Jesus to take on human flesh. This was God's amazing plan of redemption, something which succeeding Old Testament prophets faintly glimpsed and strained to understand – along, it seems, with angelic beings (see 1 Peter 1:10–12). Indeed, the whole of the Old Testament can be understood a series of shadows and pictures of what was to come in terms of Jesus' life, death and resurrection (see Hebrews 8:5; 10:1).

And here, hidden away in this obscure account of Balaam, there is another shaft of light, adding to all these other rays of revelation, foretelling the purpose of Jesus. This is laid out in his fourth oracle or declaration.

As with the previous one, this utterance from Balaam is no

longer accompanied by any divination. Quite the opposite. Balaam's unveiling of the One we recognize as Jesus is again prefaced by testifying that what he brings is a result of hearing a voice: *'the oracle of one who hears the words of God'* (24:16). He acknowledges that he has received revelation from God: *'The oracle ... of one whose eye sees clearly ... who falls prostrate, and whose eyes are opened'* (vv. 15,16).

LOCATION, LOCATION, LOCATION

Before looking at the content of this supernatural revelation, it is worth noting the scenario. We may subconsciously feel that to experience something significant from God we have got to be in a suitable place. This could be a church service or meeting, being alongside other Christians or some 'holy' place. However, with Balaam such criteria were clearly not satisfied. He was out in the open, on the edge of the desert; the smoke from those pagan sacrifices was possibly still wafting in the air. But still God broke through and touched him. Similarly, we may be standing in a train commuting to work, sitting on a park bench, or just queuing at a check-out. In any or all of these unlikely places, God can still, as it were, tap us on the shoulder. (I have personally had it happen in all three situations.)

Other accounts in the Bible also show God turning up in unexpected places. The apostle John received a mighty revelation of Jesus while on the Isle of Patmos – a penal colony. Peter experienced God's call while on the seashore – his place of work. And a woman met Jesus in a significant way while at the first century equivalent of Tesco's, drawing water from the well that everyone had to go to sooner or later – but without the clubcard!

> But still God
> broke through
> and touched him.

BALAAM'S ENCOUNTER

So what followed in terms of Balaam's vision? It was something dazzling in its content and prospect: *'A star will come out of Jacob; a sceptre will rise out of Israel'* (v. 17). Jesus, *'the light of the world'* (John 8:12), is portrayed by others in similar vein, such as Zechariah in Luke 1:78. How amazing that against this backdrop of brooding darkness, Balaam is used to declare the hope of Jesus Himself. Because when Jesus is acknowledged as being present in situations, He is seen as the mighty King of kings and Lord of lords.

THE UNSEEN JESUS

This description by Balaam of something more taking place in terms of God's intervention is a heartening picture. Jesus comes to us even in the darkest moments. Things may be at their worst or most unpromising, but He is always present. The apostle Paul received a message from God reminding him of Jesus being with him when in a storm-tossed boat that had been so pounded by the elements and for so long that the occupants had given up all hope of being saved (see Acts 27). Years before, some disciples of Jesus had been in a similar situation when Jesus came to them walking on the water (see Matthew 14:22–27).

Similarly, the two disciples walking back from Jerusalem to the village of Emmaus following the crucifixion of Jesus failed to recognize Him being present with them. They were so distraught and dragged down by hopelessness that even though Jesus Himself drew alongside, they did not realize what was happening. Only as He broke bread at the meal to which they urged Him to stay following His comprehensive Old Testament overview predicting His death and victory (I wonder if Balaam's declarations featured in this profound discourse) do we read, *'Then their eyes were opened'* (Luke 24:31). He had been with them all along, even in their emotional, spiritual and physical distress.

Luke's Gospel also records two other lesser-known characters who saw beyond their natural senses. These were the priest, Simeon, and Anna, the devout worshipper. Everyone else in the Temple at that time would simply have seen another newly born baby going through the requirements of the Levitical law. But these two saw more. Simeon declared: *'For my eyes have seen your salvation, which you have prepared in the sight of all people, a light for revelation to the Gentiles and for glory to your people Israel'* (Luke 2:30–32). Immediately following this we are told of Anna: *'Coming up to them at that very moment, she gave thanks to God and spoke about the child to all who were looking forward to the redemption of Jerusalem'* (Luke 2:38). They received revelation that the baby Jesus was God coming to this earth to bring salvation and redemption.

> He had been with them all along...

Jesus is not limited by what is happening around or within us. Nor is He restrained by other people not seeing things as we are brought to see them. Storm or prison, illness and aloneness, depression or desolation, hopelessness or disaster... He comes and shows Himself to us even when we feel we have no energy to reach out to Him. Balaam's pronouncement of Jesus being seen amongst His people, even though unheard or unperceived by the wandering Israelites at that time *'I see him, but not now; I behold him, but not near'* (v. 17), was a truth that they would one day need to grasp (see John 1:14). Likewise, we need to see this for ourselves.

HIS AUTHORITY...

More than a recognition of Jesus' future presence, Balaam also described Him as the One who would *'crush'* adversaries, see His enemies *'conquered'*, and as the *'ruler'* who would come out of Israel (vv. 17–19). All these descriptions prefigure the work of Christ in defeating the power of sin, sickness, death and hell.

Jesus' supremacy was demonstrated in His ministry. Although we read that touch and action featured on many occasions when bringing wholeness into lives, He also achieved this by simply speaking. We read that He *'rebuked'* the fever afflicting Peter's mother-in-law (Luke 4:39), *'commanded'* the evil spirit out of the demon-possessed man (Luke 8:29), directed the official *'You may go'* (John 4:50), in respect of his dying son (who was found recovered), and declared to the crippled woman, *'you are set free'* (Luke 13:12). Finally, to the very-dead-and-in-the-tomb-for-four-days Lazarus He spoke with a loud voice: *'come out!'* (John 11:43). Even the forces of nature (possibly demonically induced) were subject to the Creator's voice: *'Quiet! Be still!'* (Mark 4:39.)

Do we get 'hung up' on wanting to experience something dramatic when needing Jesus to move in our lives? Perhaps it's a case of simply hearing His voice and prayerfully agreeing with what He says. Balaam's prophetic utterance concerning the presence and power of Jesus points to the truth that sets us free (see John 8:32)

... OVER ALL

But Balaam isn't quite finished. His final words seem unconnected with all that has gone before but are, nevertheless, important. Having focused on the Children of Israel up to this point, it seems that his gaze moves off target. But it shows that God is not unaware of those around His people... and has something to speak into their situations. The people-group known as Amalek had ambushed the Israelites during their wilderness wanderings (as described in Deuteronomy 25:17,18) and would consequently perish (they were subsequently defeated by King Saul; 1 Samuel 15:2; see Deuteronomy 25:19). In contrast, the Kenites had been friendly towards, and associated with, God's people (Moses' father-in-law being from this group; see Judges 1:16). They were promised a period of security before being overcome by the power of Assyria (*'Asshur'*). The end of this declaration is obscure, referring to the end of that Assyrian empire. But the underlying message is clear. God is aware of peoples and nations, and exercising control over even the most oppressive of them (vv. 20–24). This is particularly reflected in the apostle John's description of Jesus being One whose powerful speech was like a 'sharp double-edged sword' (Revelation 1:16).

So carried by God's Spirit it seems that this fifth and closing declaration of victory is spoken without any preface or indication that Balaam is speaking what God is giving him. This may have reflected the situation described by the apostle: '... *men spoke from God as they were carried along by the Holy Spirit*' (2 Peter 1:21).

CONCLUSION

Balaam, having spoken God's heart of blessing over the people of Israel in a totally unlikely and unpromising setting, now returns home. Balak, the opposer of God's people and His purposes for them, also leaves. He had set everything up with the intention of bringing a curse, but seen and heard a totally different outcome from what he had planned. Jesus, the One who is the Victor, has indeed been seen as God's final and complete Word.

Whatever voices may be around and within us, trying to destroy what God has for us, it is Jesus who has the final say in our lives.

Luke's Gospel picks up on the way in which He talked: '*All spoke well of him and were amazed at the gracious words that came from his lips ... All the people were amazed and said to each other, "What is this teaching? With authority and power he gives orders to evil spirits and they come out!"*' (Luke 4:22a,36). These are the hallmarks of God's voice, being gracious, having authority and power, and which He wants you and I to hear over all those other voices.

FOR REFLECTION

1. Have you been through a dark experience recently? Did you know the presence of Jesus? If so, how did it help? If not, how might knowing Jesus was present with you have been of benefit?

2. What steps can we take to bring about a greater sense of the presence of Jesus when we don't feel that He is close to us?

3. The Children of Israel (and, subsequently, the two disciples on the road to Emmaus) could not see that God was involved in all that was happening around them. That only became apparent later. How important is it for us to 'hang on', believing that Jesus is with us to see us through?

4. What encouragement is there in reading that Jesus is One who has crushed and conquered our enemies, is the ruler of all and has subdued our oppressors? (See also Luke 4:16–19; Romans 16:20; Colossians 1:15–20; 2:13–15.)

5. What encouragement do you feel when reading of Jesus speaking in words described as being *gracious*, and having *authority and power*?

HEARING BUT NOT LISTENING

BIBLE READING:
Numbers 31:1–12

S at Navs are amongst the many technical innovations now forming part of our lives. Aimed at assisting motorists in driving to unfamiliar destinations, they prove extremely helpful. But not all the time. A list of over twenty black spots in the UK has now been established where instructions from the TomTom and other similar devices do not result in a positive experience. Being directed to a non-existent river crossing, taking a turning along a railway track, being wedged in narrow village streets, and pointed to one-way systems (in the wrong direction) are some of the problems they have caused. Set against these accounts are the myriad stories of drivers flagrantly ignoring this equipment, having local knowledge of better routes, causing a distraught 'voice' to issue new instructions to the recalcitrant user in a vain attempt to bring them back into line.

Balaam, the man of voices, was last seen heading back home

(Numbers 24:25). The great leader of the Israelites, Joshua, succinctly described God's view of his intervention in the history of His people: '*When Balak son of Zippor, the king of Moab, prepared to fight against Israel, he sent for Balaam son of Beor to put a curse on you. But I would not listen to Balaam, so he blessed you again and again, and I delivered you out of his hand*' (Joshua 24:9,10).

But rather like those Sat Navs, Balaam's voice was not to end in a positive result. Further references to his influence, including verses in the New Testament, draw on his actions as illustrative of how not to behave... and the severe consequences of behaving as he did.

Initially, it looked as though the danger was now over. The threat to the Israelites was no longer present, with Balak and Balaam going their separate ways. But in the very next chapter of Numbers (25), we read that internal seduction succeeded where external machinations had failed: '*While Israel was staying in Shittim, the men began to indulge in sexual immorality with Moabite women, who invited them to the sacrifices to their gods. The people ate and bowed down before these gods. So Israel joined in worshipping the Baal of Peor. And the LORD's anger burned against them*' (Numbers 25:1-3). As a consequence, God sent a plague which claimed twenty-four thousand lives, and only stopped because of the righteous anger and action of a particular priest (Numbers 25: 6-9).

BALAAM'S RETURN

Who was behind this turning from God? It is not until we read further that we find that the principal instigator of Israel's apostasy was... Balaam! Failing to destroy God's people by pronouncing curses on them, he now worked to lead them away from God through indulging in the fertility rites of Baal: '*The LORD said* to Moses: '*Take vengeance on the Midianites for the Israelites ...*' ... *They fought against Midian, as the* LORD *commanded Moses, and killed every man. ... They also killed Balaam son of Beor with the sword. ... Moses was angry with the officers of the army ... "Have you allowed all the women to live?" he asked them. "They were the ones who followed Balaam's advice and were the means of turning the Israelites away from the* LORD *in what happened at Peor, so that a plague struck the* LORD*'s people"'* (Numbers 31:1,2,7,8,14–16).

BALAAM'S ERROR
So what had happened to Balaam? Why did he, having heard the words of God and seen visions from the Almighty, end up in this ignominious way? The answer is found in the New Testament. The letters of 2 Peter and Jude, together with the Revelation of John, refer to Balaam's waywardness as a severe warning. This revolved around money. Balak had lured Balaam onto the scene by means of substantial rewards. This remained uppermost in his priorities. It seems that he reconnected with Balak on this basis to suggest another way of removing the threat which the Israelites presented. God spoke to the Christians in the church at Pergamum: '*You have people there who hold to the teaching of Balaam, who taught Balak to entice the Israelites to sin by eating food sacrificed to idols and by committing sexual immorality*' (Revelation 2:14). Jude's epistle adds this financial element: '*They have ... rushed for profit into Balaam's error*' (Jude 11).

Why did Balaam go off the rails? Why was he so drawn by temporary material gain that ended with his death, when he had been afforded glimpses of God's eternal purposes? A significant element in answering these serious questions comes back to the theme of these studies – voices. Balaam was listening to the many voices around him and choosing which to absorb and act upon.

It was such choices that specifically caused him to act in the way that he did.

It may seem over the top, but encapsulated, in a few words, our eternal destiny (not to mention our brief time on this earth) is dependent upon voices and how we respond to them.

God's voice is one that we hear and, like Balaam, to which we also have the opportunity to respond. That reference to Balaam issued by Jesus to the church at Pergamum concludes with these words: *'He who has as ear, let him hear what the Spirit says to the churches'* (Revelation 2:17; a phrase used in speaking to each of the seven churches). There is something being stressed. This is also picked up by James in his epistle: *'Do not merely listen to the word, and so deceive yourselves. Do what it says'* (James 1:22).

> Balaam was listening to the many voices around him and choosing which to absorb and act upon

PARABLE OF THE SOILS

In the light of these warnings, either Balaam didn't sense the profundity of what he was hearing (and then speaking out), or it was displaced by the voice of temptation. Perhaps it was a combination of both. Either way, the well-known parable of the sower illustrates what can take place. As has been observed by commentators, neither the sower nor the seed were actually the object of scrutiny in what was being taught by Jesus. Rather, the parable could more aptly be described as the parable of the soil.

The seed, as Jesus explained, was the word of God (Luke 8:11), with the soil depicting the hearts of the hearers. It is here that details are given regarding how people respond to God's voice.

42

HEARING BUT NOT LISTENING

The first group, likened to the pathway where the seed is trampled upon or eaten by birds, has the word taken away by the devil: '*so that they may not believe and be saved*' (v. 12). The second group looks more promising, except that having the seed fall upon rocks there is no root system. Hence, "*They believe for a while, but in the time of testing they fall away*' (v. 13). Similarly the third group have evidences of growth until the cares of this world, its riches and pleasures, choke development, so that they do not mature (v. 14). It is only the final group, '*good soil*', where God's word is retained and perseverance shown, that growth, maturity and multiplicity are achieved: '*a noble and good heart*' (v. 15).

Clearly this final 'soil' represents those who are saved, evidenced by a spiritually fruitful life. The situation regarding the initial group is also plainly stated. Their hardness of heart means they simply do not receive God's word. They may hear it audibly and understand it intellectually, but it goes no further and brings no spiritual change or life. The second soil describes those who fall away or stumble when testing or persecution arises, while the third applies to those whose maturing is suffocated by the pressures and distractions of this world. So which of these applied to Balaam? Clearly Jesus is carefully explaining a very important spiritual truth. He uses the phrase, '*He who has ears to hear, let him hear*' (v. 8), being a challenge to his hearers, and us, to understand the message and apply it in a personal way.

A DOG RETURNING TO ITS VOMIT

The verdict on Balaam, and the answer as to what kind of 'soil' he might represent, comes from those New Testament passages. The specific context of both Peter and Jude's reference to him is that of '*false prophets*' (2 Peter 2:1) and '*godless men*' (Jude 4). The former, having sandwiched Balaam in between a list of unmistakable condemnatory terms (vv. 15,16), concludes describing those of his like with a sting in the tail: *'If they have escaped the corruption of the world by knowing our Lord and Saviour Jesus Christ and are again entangled in it and overcome, they are worse off at the end than they were at the beginning. It would have been better for them not to have known the way of righteousness, than to have known it and then to turn their backs on the sacred command that was passed on to them. Of them the proverbs are true: "A dog returns to its vomit," and, "A sow that is washed goes back to her wallowing in the mud'* (vv. 20–22).

A CONTENTIOUS ISSUE

Alongside these stern verses may be brought Hebrews 6. This describes people who have *'once been enlightened, who have tasted the heavenly gift, who have shared in the Holy Spirit, who have tasted the goodness of the word of God and the powers of the coming age'* (vv. 4,5). Balaam would seem to have ticked most of these boxes. But the writer continues with a shocking pronouncement: *'... if they fall away, to be brought back to repentance, because to their loss they are crucifying the Son of God all over again and subjecting him to public disgrace'* (v. 6). In the preceding chapters the writer on no less than three occasions quotes Psalm 95:7, *'Today if you hear his voice, do not harden your hearts …'* (Hebrews 3:7,8; 3:15; 4:7) as he urges his hearers to hold onto the truth about Jesus and God, and not be pulled away as the Israelites had been when in their desert wandering.

So was Balaam at any stage a true believer in God, and is he an example of someone who is in a saving relationship that can fall away and be lost again? Did he receive God's word as being real, but then disregard it on account of hearing another voice, that of materialism? Much serious consideration has been given to these questions. Perhaps in our lack of certainty the best way of approaching this issue is to say that we should all be living careful and watchful lives as Christians, rather than presume that we can never be lost (thereby leading to possible carelessness in our walk with God). The parable of the soils reminds us of the need to, *'hear the word, retain it, and by persevering produce a crop'* (Luke 8:15).

A SECOND CHANCE

But perhaps there is a final factor to take into account. The Old Testament describes another prophetic word from God in the context of a recalcitrant hearer. Jonah may have had more going for him that Balaam, as he clearly discerned God's voice: *'The word of the LORD came to Jonah son of Amittai'* (Jonah 1:1). His response is well known. He does a runner. But God is ready for him. Swallowed by a great fish, he responds with genuine and heartfelt repentance. He acknowledges God's voice: *'In my distress I called to the LORD, and he answered me'* (Jonah 2:2). He was then unceremoniously vomited upon dry land – compare and contrast with the earlier reference to this activity!

... that life-changing word can come again...

What may then be described as the most wonderful words of Scripture in such a context are then brought: *'Then the word of the LORD came to Jonah a second time'* (Jonah 3:1).

Balaam, the man of voices, ends up having the verdict given on him as one who was lost. He never heard or seemingly wanted to hear God's voice again after his series of amazing and spiritually enlightening encounters. We can only conjecture on how different things may have been. What we do know is that God's voice is heard by those who turn to Him and that, even after wandering away, that life-changing word can come again – a second time.

FOR REFLECTION

1. *'He who has ears, let him hear'* (Matthew 11:15). What, during the time spent reading these studies, do you sense you have heard God speak or remind you of, in respect of His care for you, and His direction for your life?

2. How much do you identify with Jonah in hearing God speak, but then, like Balaam, going away from His word?

3. What encouragement is there in knowing that God doesn't give up on us and will speak a second time?

Lightning Source UK Ltd.
Milton Keynes UK
UKHW02f0010261117
313355UK00006B/132/P